BAMBOO
Architecture & Design

BAMBOO
Architecture & Design

Chris van Uffelen

BRAUN

Content

Preface

Bamboo is a giant grass that is native to all continents except Europe and Antarctica. It grows in the south of North America, in Central America and in the northern part of South America, where it can even be found on the east coast all the way up to Patagonia. In the Andes it even grows at a height of 4,700 meters above sea level, just below the snow line. In the Himalayas, bamboo can be found growing at a height of 3,800 meters above sea level. In Asia, it grows in an area that reaches from Japan, through China and India, all the way to North Australia. Furthermore, bamboo also grows in many places in Western, Central and Eastern Africa. It was scientifically documented for the first time by Carl von Linné in 1778, and today there are approximately 1,450 known types and around 130 non-woody varieties. The latter grows primarily in South America, while China has the largest variety of bamboo species, boasting over 500 different varieties.

Although not all types of bamboo are equally well suited to serve as construction material, it is traditionally used for building by all the different cultures native to the regions in which it grows. Bamboo is easily available and grows quickly; a growth rate of from ten to thirty centimeters a day is typical. Because it is mostly the lignifying type of bamboo that is used as a building material, it is usually only harvested around three years after it was planted. The natural compound material has outstanding properties: its compressive strength is equal to that of wood, stone or concrete, while its tensile strength is equal to that of steel. It varies in length from eight to fifteen meters and has a diameter from five to twelve centimeters, making it pretty much the perfect raw material for building. The Guadua angustifolia variety has a diameter of 12 centimeters and a length of 20–25 meters. The "lightweight" construction of the stem as a series of hollow chambers with nodals between them gives these 'skyscrapers' their stability. Their natural composition makes them robust and gives them a high degree of elasticity, which helps to make bamboo earthquake resistant. The smooth surface is almost like a layer of varnish and makes the stems waterproof, weatherproof and resistant to fire and chemicals. However, the stems can easily split if they are dried out, or can rot if they are exposed to too much moisture. Appropriate harvesting and drying processes can help to prevent this. The outstanding static characteristics of bamboo made it

a much-coveted material for constructing scaffolding, although this practices is now slowly being replaced by the use of industrial solutions. The use of bamboo as a building material is also decreasing and slowly beginning to disappear from large cities; although, it still enjoys great popularity in rural areas as the "poor man's wood". However, traditional building techniques are also endangered even in rural areas. Its reputation as a 'cheap' material has led to a certain amount of opposition to using bamboo as a building material in the regions where it grows. Although bamboo is not native to Europe, it is becoming evermore popular as an attractive and ecological building material in product and interior design here. Even its use as a building material is increasingly being discussed in North America and Europe; and it is not just the pioneers of lightweight building constructions, such as Richard Buckminster Fuller or Frei Otto that are interested in this subject; but also other architects that are inspired by bamboo for ecological or esthetic reasons. Today, even European architects can be found working in areas where bamboo grows, although this does involve an exchange of knowledge in both directions: new construction principles in exchange for traditional knowledge of the material.

Bamboo is also becoming more popular as a material for building large buildings. After the Expo in Hanover in 2000, everyone was fascinated by the halls built for the environmental protection agency Zeri by Columbian architect Simón Vélez, and the paper-covered Japanese Pavilion by Shigeru Ban. Various pavilions from the Shanghai Expo 2010 are presented in this book. The projects included in this volume demonstrate a wide range of projects of all sizes. Bamboo is not only used as a structural material but also often as a design element in itself. The variety of uses, functions, types of bamboo and inventive ways of using it make this book an exciting and interesting read. The compatibility of state-of-the-art technology and bamboo is demonstrated by the American inventor Thomas Alva Edison: After he had carried out more than 1,200 experiments with a wide variety of materials, he financed expeditions to collect exotic plants and later used carbonized Japanese Phyllostachys bambusoides to create filament for the electric light bulb, patented in 1881.

→ Traditional bamboo architecture in the Mekong Delta / Vietnam

Low Energy Bamboo House

AST 77 architects and engineering

Location	Rotselaar, Belgium
Completion	2011
Client	Thijs - Peeters
Type of use	Living
Gross floor area	260 m²
Bamboo used	Moso bamboo
Photos	Steven Massart

Designed by Belgian practice AST 77 the Low Energy Bamboo House is nestled within a woodland plot in Rotselaar, Belgium. The 26.3-meter-long by 4.5-meter-wide dwelling is an open volume which navigates a steep slope. The exterior is clad with bamboo poles framed with black steel structural elements. The façade treatment attempts to recede into the context of tree trunks. Strategically placed windows offer outward views and increase passive solar gain, ventilation and natural daylight. Ideal orientation within the woodland setting as well as a heat pump, floor heating and good insulation reach low energy coefficients K33 and E40. The internal organization is placed at various floor heights to interconnect upper and lower stories.

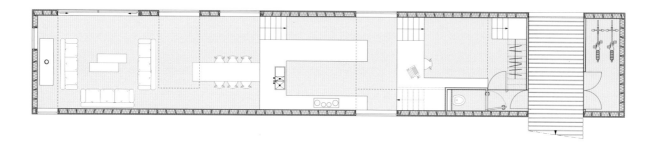

↑ Ground floor plan
↓ Building situated on a slope

↑ Front view
↓ Façade with bamboo and black steel frames

↑ Large windows provide views of tree tops
↓ Façade detail

↑ Living area
→ Building surrounded by trees

Ranch House

Galeazzo Design

Location	Caucaia do Alto, Brazil
Completion	2013
Client	Confidential
Type of use	Leisure
Gross floor area	2,800 m²
Bamboo used	Dendrocalamus giganteus, Phyllostachys pubescens
Photos	Maìra Acayaba

This small hotel has an abundance of private spaces where guests can relax in peace. An old elevator has been restored and now connects all three floors. Outside, fountains, lakes, waterfalls and a variety of gardens amplify the sense of tranquility and relaxation. The high ceilings inside are lined with bamboo. The large openings and windows, combined with the bamboo ceilings create a light-flooded bright interior that successfully combines modern design with traditional materials. The use of natural materials and neutral colors underscores the intended tranquility of the design.

↑ Interior of living area
↓ Terrace and pool

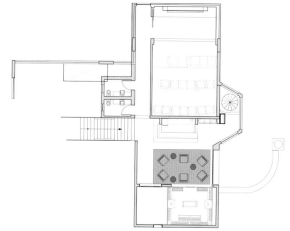

↑ Ground floor plan
→ Bamboo roof leading to entrance

↑ Bamboo roof detail
↓ Living room

↑ View through window
→ Interior with bamboo ceiling and walls

Ilha Bela House

Studio MK27 – Marcio Kogan and Diana Radomysler

Location	Ilha Bela, Brazil
Completion	2010
Client	Confidential
Type of use	Living
Gross floor area	430 m²
Bamboo used	Moso bamboo
Photos	Pedro Vannucchi

Located on the coast of São Paulo, the sole access to Ilha Bela is by boat. The island is covered by the dense Atlantic forest. The Ilha Bela House by Studio MK27 is on a beautiful beach on the northern part of the island. A stone volume divides the street and the garden. Facing the garden and visible from practically the entire house, a sculpture of Buddha sits on a specially designed space in the stone wall. The living room is on the ground floor and opens out towards both the back and front gardens. This also made it possible to establish cross ventilation in the social space, greatly improving thermal comfort. The house is structured by two lateral stone gables that form a type of porch.

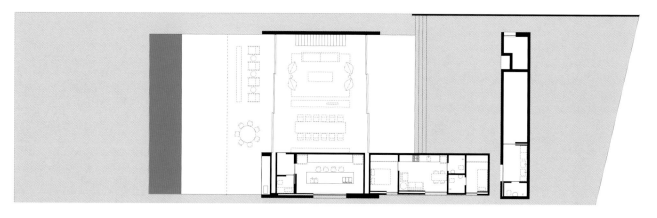

↑ Ground floor plan
↓ Night view from garden with lighting

→ Living area and pool

↑ View from garden
↓ Bamboo façade

↑ Living room opens to garden
→ Light and shadow through bamboo poles

Contemporary Hut

Galeazzo Design

Location	São Paulo, Brazil
Completion	2012
Client	Confidential
Type of use	Leisure
Gross floor area	120 m²
Bamboo used	Dendrocalamus giganteus, Phyllostachys aure, Phyllostachys pubescens
Photos	Célia Weiss

This project emphasizes the value of handmade work and sustainable construction. The hut was built with a handcraft technique using autoclaved bamboo and overlaid with piassava straw (Brazilian natural fiber) with flooring of certified wood. Outside, colored mattresses are scattered across the wooden deck, loosely surrounding a fire pit at the center. The outdoor spaces are an extension of the interior, expanding the living area and incorporating nature into the design as a whole. The construction ensures good insulation and keeps the house cool in summer and warm in winter.

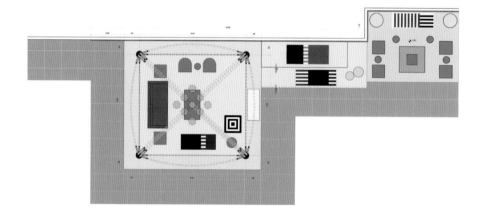

↑ Site plan
↓ Interior of hut with seating

→ Hut supported by bamboo poles

↑ Outdoor areas provide more space
↓ Interior detail

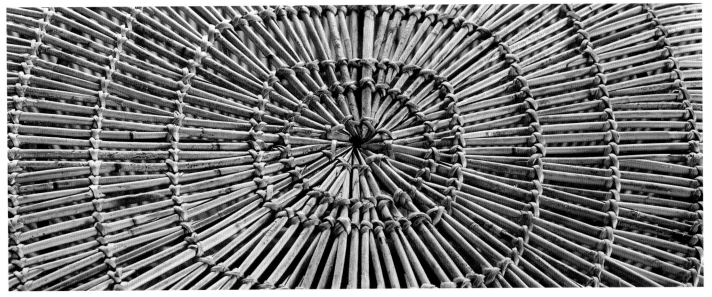

↑ Interiors made from natural materials
↓ Soapstone fire pit

Urban Cabin

Galeazzo Design

Location	São Paulo, Brazil
Completion	2011
Client	Confidential
Type of use	Leisure
Gross floor area	90 m²
Bamboo used	Dendrocalamus giganteus, Phyllostachys pubescens
Photos	Marco Antùnio

A sustainable framework of giant bamboo beams and columns was added to help the existing structure cope with the heavy load. Inside, a large circular porthole strengthens the relationship between interior and exterior and also frames the landscape, making the most of the views. The shack is a contemporary version of housing that brings back the idea of a central living space that shares a strong link with the outdoors. Outside, a stretched sail shades the large counter with tiles of different patterns. The use of bright colors contrasts the natural colors and traditional styles used inside.

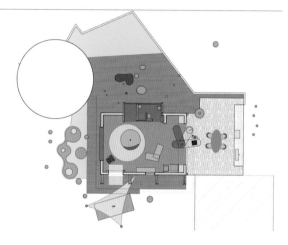

↑ Site plan
↓ Colorful façade and shaded parking space

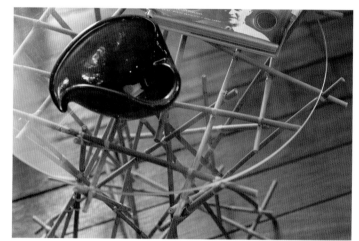

↑ Interior detail

↑ Window framed by circular book shelf
↓ Façade and bamboo supports

↑ Garden with seating

Kouk Khleang Youth Center

Komitu Architects

Location	Phnom Penh, Cambodia
Completion	2014
Clients	Cambodian Volunteers for the Society (CVS), Khmer Kampuchea Krom Human Rights and Development Association (KKKHRDA)
Type of use	Education, community center
Gross floor area	258 m²
Bamboo used	Dendrocalamus, Oxytenanthera
Photos	Montana Rakz, Gregory Pellechi (p. 26 b. r.)

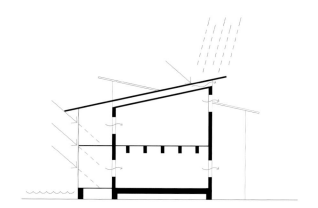

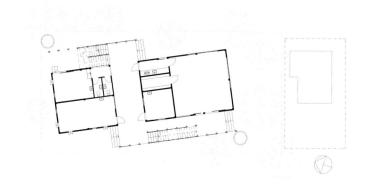

The Kouk Khleang Youth Center is a the result of a collaboration between Komitu Architects, and two Cambodian non-governmental organizations who work with the young people in Phnom Penh's poor communities. The future users played an essential role in the design process. Local students were engaged in the process and were inspired to start working on their own bamboo projects later on. The building includes spaces for education, meetings and accommodation. Bamboo is used for the load bearing structures and in the façade. The heart of the building is formed by terraces which are protected by bamboo screens. The bamboo was treated on site, only hand tools were used in the assembly and local community members were employed and trained in the construction.

↑ Ground floor plan
↓ Central terrace

↓ Bamboo structures and shading elements

← Conceptual section
↓ Front façade

↑ Oxytenanthera bamboo used in windows

Integer Bamboo House

Integer, The Oval Partnership

Location	Kunming, China
Completion	2008
Client	Hexy Horti-Expo Xing Yun Real Estate Co Ltd
Type of use	Living
Gross floor area	180 m²
Bamboo used	Laminated moso bamboo
Photos	Dr. Lin Hao, Peaker Chu (pp. 28 r., 29 a. r.)

The world's first multi-story laminated bamboo house has been completed by the research team at Integer Ltd. The bamboo house action research project is located at the Expo Integer site, in Kunming, China. The structure, the external and the internal wall panels are all made of bamboo. The bamboo structure is light and, as a result, more effective in resisting earthquakes than heavy concrete structures. The technology used in the Kunming Integer Bamboo House is based on a rain screen system and sandwich panels, which provide very high thermal insulation value. The potential of this technology is immense. It can provide an affordable and ecological way of building for new townships and villages in China.

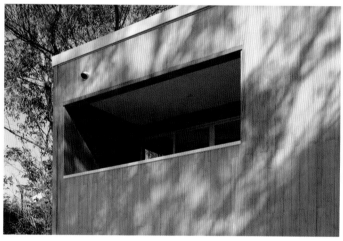

↑ Façade view from garden
↓ Section

↑ Interior clad with bamboo

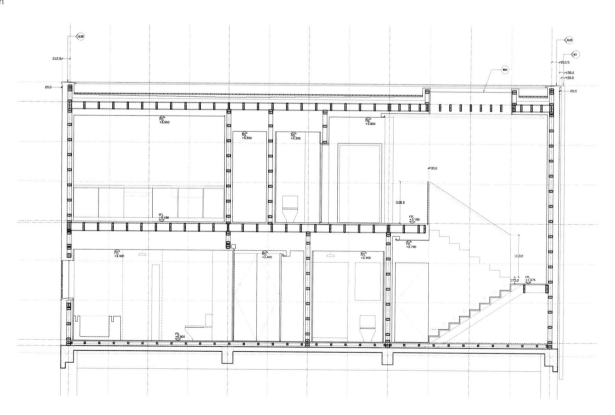

↑ Upper level entrance
↓ Balcony on first floor

↑ Living room with bamboo furniture

Harvest Pavilion

Vector Architects

Location	Kunshan, China
Completion	2012
Client	Kunshan City Investment Company
Type of use	Leisure
Gross floor area	150 m²
Bamboo used	Laminated bamboo slate
Photos	Shu He (pp. 32 b., 33 a. l.), Su Shengliang
	(pp. 31, 32 a., 33 a. r.), Zhi Xia (p. 30)

Situated on an eco-farm alongside the Yang Cheng Lake, Kunshan, this project consists of four small-scale public buildings: club house, harvest pavilion, botanical showroom, and information center. The harvest pavilion appears as a simple, light, and translucent cuboid, with a horizontal thin plate hovering at the top, parallel with the horizon in the distance. The projecting roof cantilevers out at various depths. The space below becomes a transition zone from the interior to the exterior, blurring the boundaries between the two and casting a pleasant shadow on the ground.

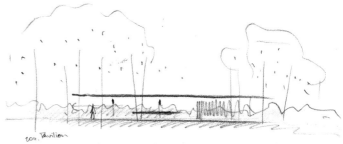

↑ Section
↓ Interior space in sunlight

↑ Sketch
→ Light and shadow through bamboo louvers

↑ View from roadside
↓ Pavilion surrounded by fields

↑ Pavilion at night
↗ Entrance area

KPMG-CCTF Community Center

Integer, The Oval Partnership

Location	Pengzhou, China
Completion	2010
Client	KPMG China / CCTF
Type of use	Community center
Gross floor area	450 m²
Bamboo used	Laminated moso bamboo
Photos	Li Zhou

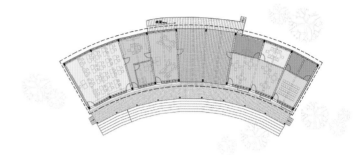

In partnership with China Children and Teenagers' Fund (CCTF) and Chengdu Women's Federation, KPMG China built this green community center in Cifeng Village as part of efforts to renovate the earthquake-devastated region and promote the development of the local rural communities. The design makes excellent use of local materials and passive systems to create an environmentally sustainable building. The 450-square-meter community center is used for local children's extracurricular activities and hosts vocational classes. The project has advanced sustainable rural community development and will serve as a paragon for improving sustainable construction, educational, cultural and recreational facilities in rural communities.

↑ Front and rear elevations
↓ Semi-open space with painted straw panel walls

↓ Bamboo structure and cladding

← Ground floor plan
↓ Bird's-eye view of KPMG-CCTF Community Center

↑ Public space with bamboo roof

Vietnam Pavilion at Expo 2010

Vo Trong Nghia Architects

Location Shanghai, China
Completion 2010
Client VEFAC (Vietnam Exhibition and Fair Center)
Type of use Exhibition
Gross floor area 915 m²
Photos Phan Quang, courtesy of the architects (pp. 36 a., 37 b.)

The motto of this expo was "Better city, better life", so the focus was on sustainable development. For developing countries, including Vietnam, the participants were presented with ordinary warehouses to use for their pavilions. The challenge was to transform the warehouse into an eye-catching pavilion where cultural exchanges could take place. Bamboo was chosen as the main material for the renovation to express the Vietnamese spirit of friendliness, durability and sustainability by the usage. The bamboo has been given an arched structure to create a wavy surface; this reduces the heat gain from sunlight. For the interior, vertical bamboo structures create an inner lining giving the impression of being in a bamboo forest.

↑ Entrance to pavilion
↓ Courtyard with bamboo façade

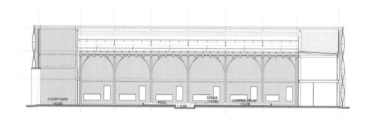

↑ Section

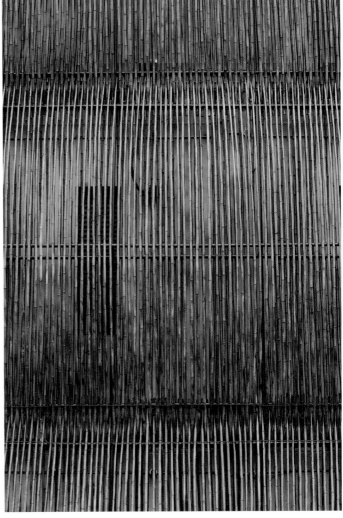

↑ Bamboo construction detail
↓ Interior with vertical bamboo structures

↑ Façade

Madrid Pavilion at Expo 2010

AZPML

Location	Shanghai, China
Completion	2010
Client	Madrid Global Foundation
Type of use	Culture, leisure
Gross floor area	2,800 m²
Bamboo used	Eko Bamboo floor on 4 cm MDF panels
Photos	Emilio P. Soiztua.

The Madrid Pavilion applies strategies originally developed for Carabanchel Social Housing. The Madrid Pavilion incorporates diverse program requirements, and accommodates different user groups. The space is divided into public spaces for exhibition visitors and professional areas, spread across five levels, and including the roof. Visitors enter the exhibition via an escalator leading from outside to the fourth floor, where the exhibition begins. This floor is designed as a promenade which descends directly into a large central atrium space. The pavilion is enclosed with bamboo louvers mounted on folding frames. The skin is configured to provide passive energy control.

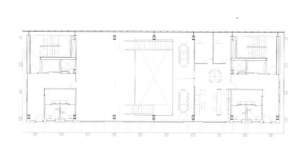

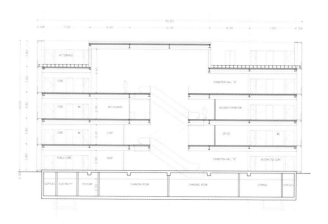

↑ First floor plan
↓ Terrace with seating

↑ Section
→ Bamboo façade mounted on folding frames

MADRID
马德里

↑ Building entrance at night
↓ General view

↑ Atrium and bamboo louvers as seen from inside
→ Stairs and façade detail

Indian Pavilion at Expo 2010

Sanjay Prakash & Associates, Pradeep Sachdeva Design Associates

Location	Shanghai, China
Completion	2010
Client	India Trade Promotion Organization
Bamboo design	Simón Vélez
Design	Design C
Type of use	Exhibition
Gross floor area	2,800 m²
Bamboo used	Moso bamboo
Photos	Pradeep Sachdeva

This large bamboo dome uses over 12 kilometers of bamboo in total. The bamboo stalks were treated with boric borax and then bent in a factory. The arches comprise 36 'ribs' each made of six interconnected bamboo stalks. The entire dome is covered with an innovative triple-layered geo-fabric membrane for growing plants. Inside, the striking structure is illuminated, making the bamboo stalks glow almost green.

↑ Bamboo roof construction
↓ Roof construction drawing

↑ Detail of bamboo support system

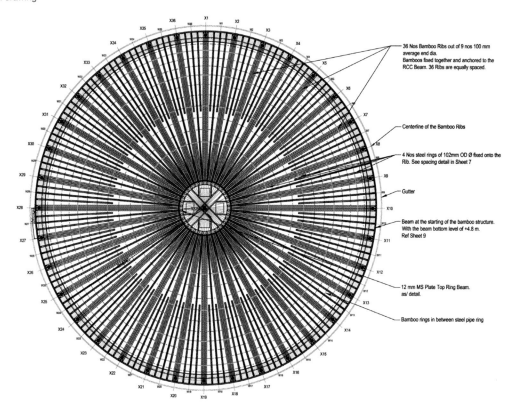

36 Nos Bamboo Ribs out of 9 nos 100 mm average end dia.
Bamboos fixed together and anchored to the RCC Beam. 36 Ribs are equally spaced.

Centerline of the Bamboo Ribs

4 Nos steel rings of 102mm OD Ø fixed onto the Rib. See spacing detail in Sheet 7

Gutter

Beam at the starting of the bamboo structure. With the beam bottom level of +4.8 m. Ref Sheet 9

12 mm MS Plate Top Ring Beam. as/ detail.

Bamboo rings in between steel pipe ring

↑ Illuminated interior
↓ Exterior of pavilion during exhibition

↑ Entrance gate to exhibition area

Norway Pavilion at Expo 2010

Helen&Hard

Location	Shanghai, China
Completion	2010
Client	Innovation Norway
Type of use	Exhibition and business center
Gross floor area	2,800 m²
Bamboo used	Laminated bamboo plates
Photos	John E Kroll (pp. 44 a., 46 a., 47 a. r.), Patrick Wack

With the theme of the Expo 2010 in Shanghai in mind, "Better City, Better Life", the project aimed to extend the life of the pavilion through after-use. This was done by creating a looser constellation of self-sustained components; a field of 'trees' which could easily be erected, dismantled and transformed. The trees were assembled into a sensory and multifunctional 'forest'. After the Expo, each individual tree would be reused as a social meeting place. Each tree comprises a CNC cut and milled laminated timber. To avoid the separation between interior and exterior, and between the architecture and the exhibition design, the architects extended the construction with a layer of CNC cut bamboo plywood plates. The bamboo layer integrates all technical infrastructure and ventilation, while creating the exhibition landscape.

↑ Interior | → Exploded axonometric view and section
↓ 'Fjordwall' made of CNC cut bamboo | →→ Exhibition area

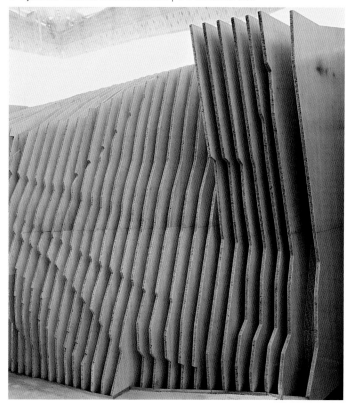

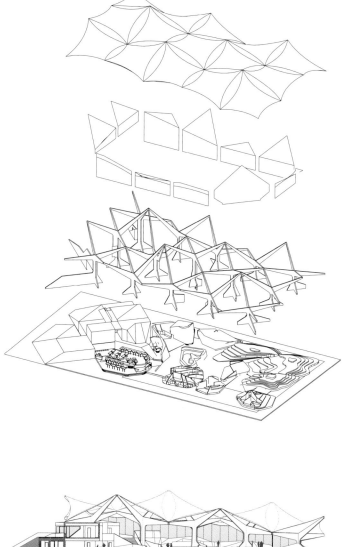

↑ Illuminated at night
↓ Roof shades entrance area

↑ Exterior with lighting
↗ Exhibition area at night

Bug Dome

Casagrande Laboratory

Location Shenzhen, China
Completion 2009
Client SZHK Biennale, curator Ou Ning
Type of use Public space
Gross floor area 120 m²
Bamboo used Shezhuan bamboo
Photos Nikita Wu

This design is inspired by insects. The bamboo construction methods are based on local knowledge from rural Guanxi brought into the city by migrating construction workers. The space was used during the SZHK Biennale for underground bands, poetry reading, discussions, karaoke and as a lounge for the workers from the neighboring camp. After the Biennale the Bug Dome will act as an un-official social club for workers from the Chinese countryside. The cocoon is a weak retreat for the modern man to escape from the strength of the exploding urbanism in the heart of Shenzhen. It is a shelter to protect the industrial insects from the elements of un-nature.

↑ Pavilion in context
↓ Sketch

↑ Entrance with greenery
→ Interior view

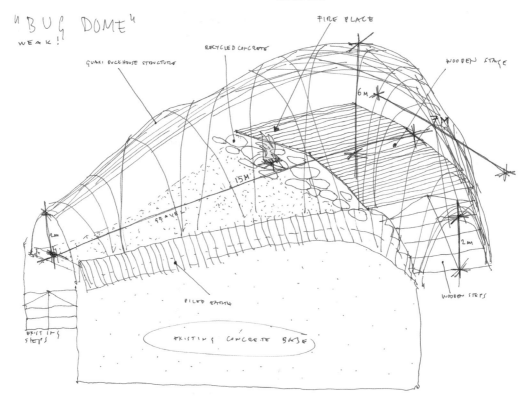

↑ General view
↓ Entrance area

↑ Night view
↗ Interior

N4+ Gluebam House

Advanced Architecture Lab [AaL]

Location	Wuhan, China
Completion	2012
Client	Advanced Architecture Lab [AaL]
Type of use	Prototype
Gross floor area	60 m^2
Bamboo used	Glue laminated bamboo
Photos	Li Xiao

This construction uses a glued bamboo prefabricated construction system developed by the Advanced Architecture Lab (AaL), together with the bamboo institute of the Chinese Academy of Forestry. The gluebam project is a long-term research project, carried out at the Huazhong University of Science and Technology's Advanced Architecture Lab. The aim of the project is to establish a method of application for this material by designing a housing project. N4+ is a house built using the gluebam technique. Completed in just 25 days, the house is a prototype based on the concept of mass production and fabrication.

↓ Interior with gluebam walls and furniture

← Axonometric diagram
↑ Terrace and interior with lighting

↑ Terrace and trees
↓ Pattern of light and shadow through front façade

WFH House

Arcgency

Location	Wuxi, China
Completion	2012
Client	worldFLEXhome
Type of use	Living
Gross floor area	180 m²
Bamboo used	Oiled bamboo LamelPlank
Photos	Jens Markus Lindhe

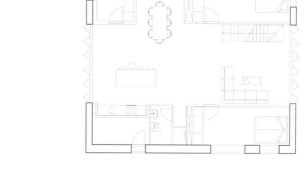

Built of old shipping containers, this house can be transported by land and sea. It uses less energy than it produces and online customization-tools even give clients the chance to create their own version of the house in terms of layout, size, façade and interior. The house can be designed to adapted to local challenges such as climatic or earthquake issues. Bamboo has been selected as the main material for this house due to its potential as a sustainable material and because it grows fast and is very easily available. The "Flex space" is the heart of the house. It contains the living room, kitchen and can be used for multiple purposes.

↓ Façade under construction

← Ground floor plan
↑ Construction phase

↑ Interior view from upper floor
↓ Building covered in bamboo façade

Bamboo Courtyard Teahouse

HWCD

Location	Yangzhou, China
Completion	2012
Client	Construction Bureau of the Economy and Technology Development District, Yangzhou
Type of use	Teahouse
Gross floor area	400 m²
Bamboo used	Mao bamboo
Photos	T+E

The focal point of this teahouse is its courtyard, which uses bamboo to create an interesting play of vertical and horizontal lines. Traditionally, Yangzhou courtyards are formed with inward-facing pavilions, creating an internal landscape space. The bamboo courtyard was designed from a basic square footprint, fragmented into small spaces to create an internal landscape area. Each of the spaces offers views of the surrounding lake. The simple form illustrates the harmonious blend of architecture and nature. The pocket of voids improves natural ventilation within the bamboo courtyard while the thick brick wall retains heat in winter, reducing the dependency on mechanical heating and cooling systems.

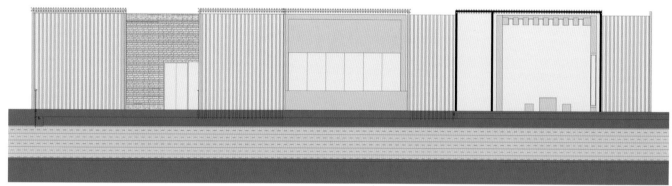

↑ Section
↓ Interior with bamboo stems hanging from ceiling

↓ Ground floor plan

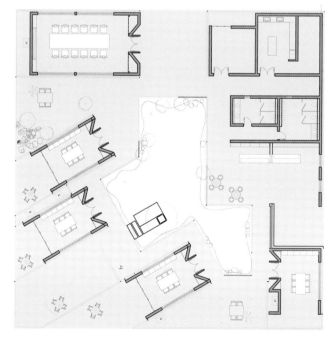

↑ Window behind bamboo stems
↓ Courtyard with lighting at night

↑ Seating
↓ Courtyard characterized by bamboo, water and greenery

↑ Teahouse shines out at night
↗ Atmosphere at dawn

A Forest for a Moon Dazzler

Benjamin Garcia Saxe

Location	Guanacaste, Costa Rica
Completion	2010
Client	Helen Saxe
Type of use	Living
Gross floor area	100 m²
Photos	Andres Garcia Lachner

This small house in the forest is designed to reflect its surroundings. The inside is like a forest within a forest, slender bamboo stems filter the light and give the feel of walking through trees. The interior furnishings, such as the closets and kitchen walls were built from trees on the site, which makes every piece unique and adds to the natural feel of the house. The bamboo used was cut from a family farm during full moon and then soaked in diesel in order to protect it from the elements, before being dried naturally beneath the shade of the trees. The bamboo stems were later cut into 15-centimeter pieces and finished with varnish. The foundations are of poured concrete and the main columns and beams are of steel, bought from a local hardware store.

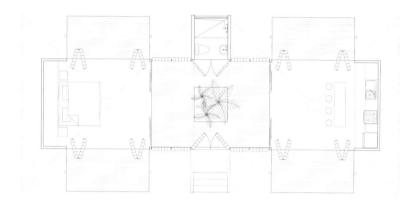

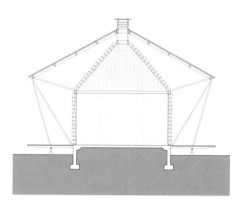

↑ Ground floor plan
↓ House surrounded by plants

↗ Section

↑ Interior with natural materials
↓ Bamboo façade

↑ Bamboo stems cut into pieces
↓ Sunlight passing through bamboo façade

↑ Entrance area
↓ House illuminated at night

Zoo Parking Lot

HPP Architekten

Location	Leipzig, Germany
Completion	2011
Client	Zoo Leipzig GmbH
Type of use	Parking lot
Gross floor area	27,500 m²
Bamboo used	Colombian guadua bamboo
Photos	PUNCTUM/B. Kober, Sigurd Steinprinz (p. 66)

The bamboo façade is the motif of both the parking garage constructed in 2004 and the extension completed in 2011. The shell lends the large garages a hint of the exotic world of the zoo. Several thousand quick-growing bamboo stalks from Columbia were arranged in rows with an axial distance of 16 centimeters. Together, the two parking garages offer about 1,336 parking spaces. The independent extension features distinctive undulations along both lengths of the façade, which help to move the building's function into the background. The bamboo façade also minimizes noise emissions, allows for ventilation and natural lighting. As a 'fifth façade', the roof surface contains extensive greenery and is used for the capture of rainwater.

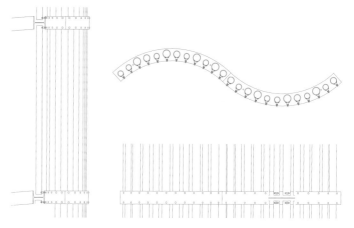

← Play of light and shadow | ↑ Façade detail
↓ Floor plan extension | → Wavy bamboo façade

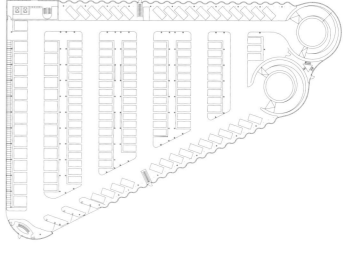

↑ Animal footprints lead the way
↓ West view of both parking garages

↑ Foyer of extension
↗ North elevation of parking garage constructed in 2004

Bamboo Symphony

MA (Manasaram Architects)

Location	Bangalore, India
Completion	2010
Client	Neelam Manjunath
Type of use	Office
Gross floor area	210 m²
Bamboo used	Bambusa bambos, Dendrocalamus strictus
Photos	Neelam Manjunath (p. 68 b.), Krishnau Chaterjee

Bamboo Symphony was built by the office of architect Neelam Manjunath. Built on a tight budget using stone, bamboo, compressed earth blocks, and debris, this is a zero energy development. The arrangement of the columns in Bamboo Symphony appears haphazard, although they are all structurally relevant. The roof was allowed to define its own shape naturally like a fabric. Visitors are greeted by a Zen water-body over a rainwater tank. The office is built around a lotus pond, which serves as a catchment area for rainwater. The waterfall creates a soothing ambience and helps maintain the humidity and prevent the bamboo from cracking.

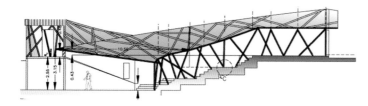

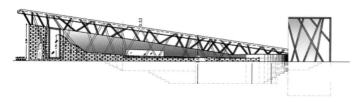

↑ South and north elevations
↓ Exterior view at night

↑ Reflection of bamboo poles

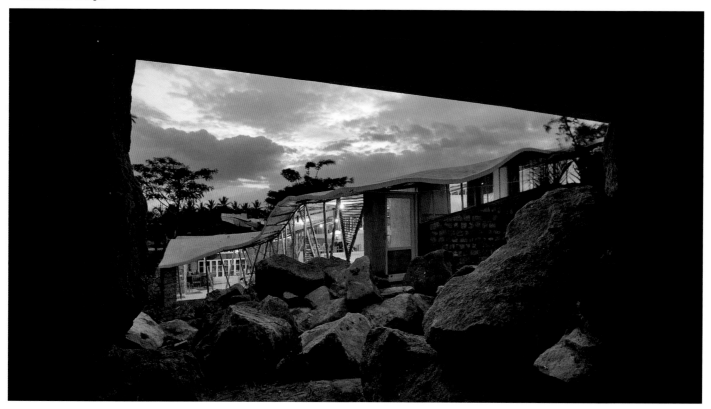

↑ Reception area
↓ Computer room with bamboo furniture

↑ Office building arranged around lotus pond

House of Five Elements

MA (Manasaram Architects)

Location	Bangalore, India
Completion	2009
Client	Neelam Manjunath
Type of use	Living
Gross floor area	1,118 m²
Bamboo used	Bambusa bambos, Dendrocalamus strictus
Photos	Neelam Manjunath (p. 71 a. l.), Krishnau Chaterjee

This house is designed with the five elements of nature in mind and caters to the three faculties of man: physical, psychological and spiritual. The spaces inside the house are peaceful and flow into each other. All the functional areas are arranged around a two-level courtyard that opens out to the sky. Bamboo is used in the walls, columns, beams and roofs. The bamboo roof is a double-curved shell on two curved bamboo beams and supported by bamboo columns. A solar/wind hybrid system is installed so that the house can go off-grid in the future.

↑ House illuminated at night
↓ Façade with bamboo elements

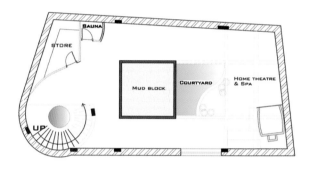

↑ Basement plan

↑ Seating around courtyard
↓ First floor with bamboo supports

↑ Courtyard with swimming pool

House by the Bamboo Grove

Pradeep Sachdeva Design Associates

Location   Gurgaon, India
Completion   2009
Client   Pradeep Sachdeva
Roof design   Simón Vélez
Type of use   Living
Gross floor area 200 m²
Bamboo used   Bambusa balcooa
Photos   Somendra Singh

This weekend home is located in Sadrana village, on an 6.000 square-meter plot surrounded by fields of seasonal crops and marigolds. The architect is also the client, and he wanted to build a house that would be versatile enough to house both large gatherings of friends and family and also be intimate enough to spend some time alone. To achieve this, the house has an open-plan arrangement with a large living and dining area which extends out to a deep verandah. The kitchen is separate from the main house, connected by a covered passage with large windows that overlook fields of mariegold flowers. This completes the picture of country style living with a patio between the house and the kitchen where meals are served in winter.

↑ Bamboo construction detail
↓ Exterior and garden

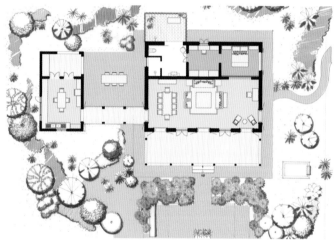

↑ Ground floor plan

↑ Building illuminated at night
↓ Terrace with seating

↑ Weekend house in the country
↓ Dining area

↑ Bamboo ceiling seen from below
→ Bedroom interior

BMW Guggenheim Lab

Atelier Bow-Wow

Location	Mumbai, India
Completion	2012
Client	Solomon R. Guggenheim Museum
Type of use	Mobile laboratory
Gross floor area	182 m²
Photos	Solomon R. Guggenheim Foundation

The BMW Guggenheim Lab is a mobile laboratory dedicated to investigating various issues related to city life. The first lab building was designed using carbon-reinforced-plastic. It was later decided that a second lab building would be constructed in Mumbai using local materials and technologies. The event organizers requested that the lab building be a freestanding structure: they wanted an itinerant space that could be moved to a new location every week. To achieve these objectives, the architects designed a structure composed of longitudinal units and truss beam units, all of which fit onto the back of a flatbed truck. To prevent the bamboo rods from splitting along the grain, the architects filled them with synthetic resin cement where they were bolted.

↑ Exhibition space surrounded by trees
↓ Sectional perspective

↑ Workshop at traveling lab location

↑ Entire view of pavilions
↓ Spaces for workshops

Oceanique Hotel Restaurant

Sanjay Puri Architects

Location	Salcete, India
Completion	2009
Client	Pearls Infrastructure
Type of use	Restaurant
Gross floor area	200 m²
Bamboo used	Bambusa balcooa
Photos	Vinesh Gandhi

A series of fluid spaces, each with their own identity created by a judicious mix of forms, materials and lighting, transform this rather staid 50-room hotel into a boutique resort with every space offering a different experience. A restaurant towards one end of the lobby is created from thin bamboo screens that undulate across the varying heights unifying the space, making it appear larger and modern. Oceanique Hotel Restaurant has undergone a complete transformation, to become a series of experiences.

↑ Atmosphere created by natural colors
↓ Bamboo-clad walls and ceiling

↓ Restaurant with seating

← Site plan of hotel and restaurant
↓ Seating for guests

↑ Light permeates bamboo ceiling

Bamboo Restaurant at Greenville

DSA+s

Location	West Jakarta, Indonesia
Completion	2010
Client	Yeye
Type of use	Restaurant
Gross floor area	148 m²
Bamboo used	Yellow and petung bamboo
Photos	Fernando Gomulya

This project is located in the Tanjung Duren area, near the Greenville housing complex in West Jakarta. It is located on one of the main streets in the Tanjung Duren area. The owner of the site commissioned the architects to build a Japanese noodle restaurant on tight budget and within a limited time frame. The architects chose bamboo as the main material for the restaurant. The design of the restaurant was inspired by an umbrella. The restaurant comprises a series of umbrellas that overlap to form a roof. Rainwater is channeled from the roof to the ground via a pipe at the center. The bamboo umbrellas not only give the restaurant a striking appearance, but also protect customers from the sun and rain.

↑ Giant bamboo umbrellas protect from sun and rain
↓ Front view

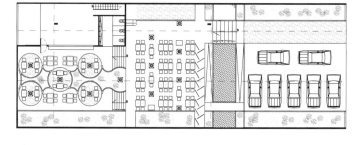

↑ Ground floor plan
→ Seating for guests

↑ Roof detail
↓ Dining area

↑ Lighting at night
↗ Bamboo support

Bamboo Gateway

Bamboo DNA

Location	Stradbally, Ireland
Completion	2009
Client	Electric Picnic
Type of use	Pavilion
Gross floor area	64 m²
Bamboo used	Guadua angustifolia
Photos	Gerard Minakawa

The Bamboo Gateway served as both a grand entrance and pavilion to Body & Soul, a special area of the Electric Picnic festival held in Stradbally, Ireland every year. It is also a permanent installation used by the landowner for various other events including horse shows. The bamboo chosen is Guadua angustifolia imported from Colombia, combined with round stones quarried from the site as well as cut limestone blocks from the old walls of the estate. The entire structure was built by a crew of eight people and took three weeks to complete. Festival volunteers also contributed to the project and were trained onsite during the building process.

↑ Illuminated at night
↓ Curved roof on bamboo supports

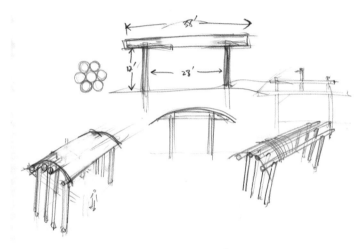

↑ Sketches

↑ Base detail
↓ Entire view

↑ Bamboo construction

Think Green – Bamboo Block House

Studio Cardenas Conscious Design

Location	Milan, Italy
Completion	2010
Client	Think Green
Type of use	Prototype
Gross floor area	12 m²
Bamboo used	Guadua angustifolia
Photos	Danilo Borrelli

A key aspect of this project is the development of a design that is aligned with nature, and that works with, rather than against, its surroundings. The use of bamboo as the main material reinforces this intention. The amount of energy used during the construction was kept to a minimum as the bamboo was grown locally and only needed to be transported from the plantation to the site. The transfer of knowledge is part of the design, the project is a kit instead rather than an architectural object itself. The kit includes a users manual that considers topics such as the choice of the plant, production and maintenance.

↑ Bamboo wall detail
↓ Bamboo house used as art gallery

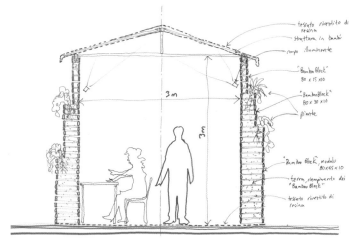

↑ Sketch by Mauricio Cardenas

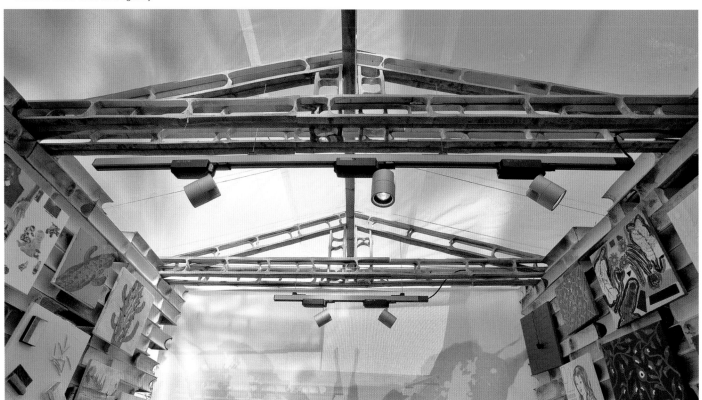

↑ Greenery on bamboo walls

↑ Flowers growing on façade

↓ Main view

Boo Tech Eco Dome

Studio Cardenas Conscious Design

Location	Milan, Italy
Completion	2009
Client	Interni Design Energies
Type of use	Exhibition pavilion
Gross floor area	18 m²
Bamboo used	Guadua angustifolia
Photos	Danilo Borrelli (pp. 88 a. r., 89 a. r.), Andres Otero

The development of a symbiosis between nature and technology is a key aspect of this design: bamboo, steel, neoprene, earth and textile work together to create a light contemporary structure. The same bamboo used in the previous pavilion was reused, cut into slats connected by steel and neoprene joints to create a complex geodesic geometry with amazing static properties, lightness, versatility and modernity. The entire construction was carried out using a dry mounting technique that requires no perforation or reinforcement.

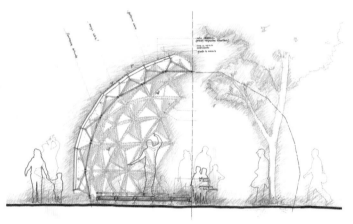

↑ Sketch by Mauricio Cardenas
↓ Construction detail

↑ Connection of steel and bamboo

↑ Seating with atmosphere like under a tree
↓ Geometry of dome orientates on Renaissance buildings

↑ Dome at dawn

Garden Terrace Miyazaki

Kengo Kuma & Associates

Location	Miyazaki, Japan
Completion	2012
Client	Ceremony Miyazaki
Type of use	Leisure
Gross floor area	4,562 m²
Bamboo used	Phyllostachys bambusoides
Photos	Fujinari Miyazaki

This hotel was built on a vast site near the JR Miyazaki station, where a factory once stood. Houses and apartments spread out in no particular order around the hotel. The building houses guest rooms, a banquet room, and restaurants, all arranged around an inner courtyard. The loosely sloped roof was the result of the functions beneath. It wraps the entire building – a two-story structure under the deep eaves. The courtyard is characterized by the use of bamboo and water features, which together create a tranquil environment.

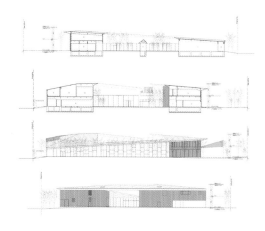

↑ Ground and first floor plans
↓ Entrance area

↑ Sections
→ Bamboo façade

↑ View to inner courtyard with water feature and living bamboo
↓ Front of building with bamboo façade

↑ Dining area
↗ Interior with bamboo ceiling

Bamboo Forest & Huts with Water

Ryuichi Ashizawa Architects & associates

Location	Osaka, Japan
Completion	2009
Client	Aqua Metropolis Osaka 2009 Executive Committee
Planning partners	Hirokazu Toki, Takashi Manda
Type of use	Temporary event space
Gross floor area	1,028 m²
Bamboo used	Phyllostachys bambusoides
Photos	Kaori Ichikawa

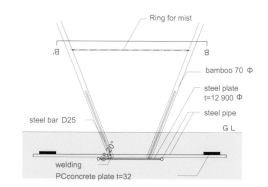

The intention of Bamboo Forest was to create a space using just one material. Constructed as part of a student workshop, the design utilizes 2,500 bamboo stems, resulting in a structure composed of eleven bamboo trunks arranged radially to form a grid pattern. There is no concrete foundation, the 24 bamboo trunks are joined by an iron plate, growing up radially from the ground. The structure is balanced, joined to form a triangular radial shape spanning 60 centimeters and connected at the tip, bending to form a curved space. The architects believe that it is possible to improve the natural surrounding through architecture. At the end of its natural cycle, this urban space was given a new purpose, a space changed by people and its organic structure.

↑ Section
↓ Space covered by Bamboo Forest & Folded-Plate Hut

↓ Architectural model

← Base section
↓ Bamboo Forest

↑ Open space under Bamboo Forest

Jugetsudo Kabukiza

Kengo Kuma and Associates

Location	Tokyo, Japan
Completion	2013
Client	Maruyama Nori
Type of use	Tearoom
Gross floor area	127 m²
Bamboo used	Japanese timber bamboo
Photos	Takumi Ota

Located on the fifth floor of the Ginza Kabukiza Theater, the Jugetsudo Kabukiza tearoom serves green teas and Japanese-style sweets. The tearoom has an area of 120 square meters and is entirely covered with bamboo. Bamboo stems are arranged at various angles and serve to separate the retail and dining areas. More than 3,000 bamboo stems have been used, creating continuity between the interior design and exterior appearance. The layered arrangement and careful division of the space create the feeling of walking through a bamboo grove, as well as creating a dynamic play of light and shadow that helps to enliven the interior.

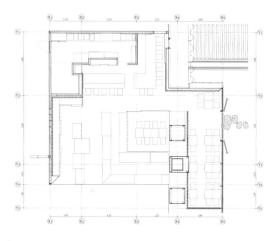

↑ Floor plan
↓ Bamboo stems create a play of light and shadow

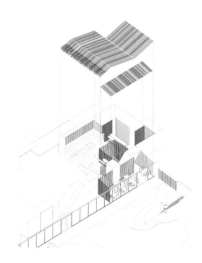

↑ Axonometry

↑ Seating with view of garden
↓ Interior covered with bamboo

↑ Interior partitioned by bamboo stems
↓ Tearoom service counter

日本茶喫茶・茶葉の店

寿月堂

↑ View from garden

Sendero Interpretativo del Bosque de Bambú

Ojtat Creatividad Regenerativa

Location	Puebla, Mexico
Completion	2012
Client	Secretaria de Sustentabilidad y Ordenamiento Territorial de Puebla
Type of use	Park
Gross floor area	3,493 m²
Bamboo used	Guadua angustifolia
Photos	Samanta Pratt Limon

Ojtat is an architectural firm that encourages the construction of sustainable cities. One of their initiatives is to create 'Urban Bamboo Forests' as a strategy to increase the availability of water, oxygen, soil and raw materials. They created their first bamboo forest in Puebla. One of the main intentions of this project is to integrate bamboo into the urban environment. This forest contains 22 bamboo species and has two main trails: one on the ground and one above ground. The path at ground level leads visitors to plazas, meditation sites and bird observatories. The project successfully demonstrates that bamboo can be used as a structural element and can be used to replace other materials such as concrete and steel.

↑ Elevation and plan
↓ Bridge from below

↑ Park with living bamboo
↓ Bamboo foundations and supports

↑ Bamboo bridge and living bamboo
↓ Black steel structural system

↑ Great bamboo corridor
→ Connection detail

Habitat Initiative Cabo Delgado

Ziegert | Roswag | Seiler Architekten Ingenieure

Location	Various locations, Mozambique
Completion	2010
Client	Aga Khan Foundation, Mozambique
Type of use	Preschools, community centers
Gross floor area	1,100 m²
Photos	Paula Holtz

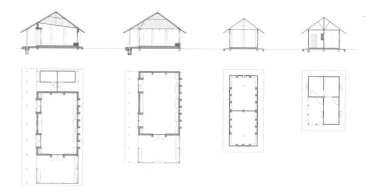

For this initiative eleven new preschools and community buildings were erected from earth and bamboo in the country's poor northern region. The schools were built to exhibit an improved construction method that incorporates and develops both local craft skills and materials. One of the project's most notable design innovations are the roof trusses, which are developed out of thin regional bamboo, and can span six meters without any support. These are formed using simple dowel connections, which are tied together with wire. The schools are designed to showcase improvements to the traditional building process and to serve as models for future housing concepts.

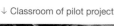

↓ Classroom of pilot project

← Sections and ground floor plans of various building types
↑ Roof construction of basic school type

↑ Bamboo truss and palm thatch
↓ General view of pilot project

Favelous 963

Ifigeneia Dilaveraki, Conbam, Elena Goray

Location	Amsterdam, The Netherlands
Completion	2013
Client	Mediamatic Fabriek
Type of use	Restaurant
Gross floor area	72 m²
Bamboo used	Dark split bamboo
Photos	Arne Kuilman (pp. 106 b. l., 107 b.), Thomas Huisman

Favelous 963 is an initiative by an interdisciplinary group of people who wanted to create a pop-up restaurant in a vacant building that was originally used for the production of train wagons. The structure needed to be lightweight, easy to assemble and made out of natural and second-hand materials. Bamboo elements interlace in different directions and densities in order to meet to structural and daylight requirements. The structure was built in just three days using 900 meters of split bamboo, 600 meters of black rope and 300 meters of waste bicycle tires.

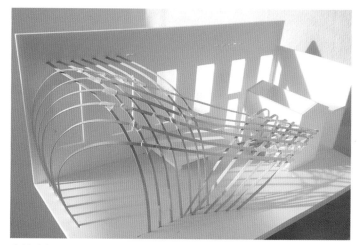

↑ Model scale 1:30
↓ Seating area for guests

↓ Play of light and shadows

← Plan of ground connections
↓ Entrance at night with lighting

↑ Bamboo detail

Cob and Bamboo School Building

Ziegert | Roswag | Seiler Architekten Ingenieure

Location   Sheikupura, Pakistan
Completion   2012
Client   Tipu Sultan Merkez
Type of use   School
Gross floor area 650 m²
Photos   Courtesy of the architects

This two-story bamboo school was built for a privately initiated, rural school and development project and helps to promote local traditions, reduce reliance on expensive products from outside the region and to develop natural material and economic cycles. The first floor is built using the wattle-and-daub method; the light bamboo structure is filled with earth and covered with a surrounding bamboo weave serving as a sunshade. The upper rooms are connected via a two-story bamboo veranda, which can be used as an extended classroom. It protects the earth walls against rain while shading the interior spaces. Ceilings and roofs are constructed using a system of triple-layer bamboo beams, joined with simple knots and steel rods and covered with a layer of earth.

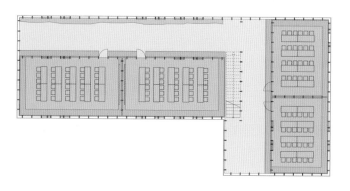

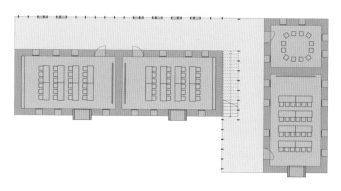

↑ Ground floor plan
↓ Ground floor classroom

↑ First floor plan

↑ View from outside campus
↓ Construction supported by bamboo poles

↑ Porch on first floor
↓ Seating niche

↑ Porches
→ Bamboo frame with earth infill

Abu Hindi Primary School

ARCò - architettura e cooperazione

Location	Wadi Abu Hindi, Palestine
Completion	2010
Client	Vento di Terra Onlus NGO
Type of use	School
Gross floor area	240 m²
Bamboo used	Phragmites australis
Photos	Andrea&Magda Photographers, courtesy of the architects (p. 113 b.)

Environmental strategies such as thermal mass and cross ventilation have been used to create a comfortable space in what was before merely an iron-sheet shelter. The technique used employs a replica system and arose as a solution to design constraints, including not being permitted to increase the size of the existing structure, and the necessity of maintaining the iron sheet. A new wall of earth and straw has been built using the existing galvanized iron sheet, with wood and bamboo as permanent shuttering. An extra bamboo layer outside protects the structure from the sun and gives the building a striking new façade. Bamboo was chosen as it is an extremely flexible material that is easily available.

↑ Classroom with alternation of plastering and bamboo
↓ Interior wall with white plastering

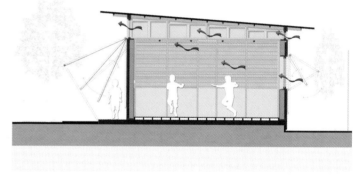

↑ Section

↑ Building surrounded by mountains
↓ Bamboo rear façade

↑ School at beginning of lessons

Family House

Atelier Sacha Cotture

Location	Paranaque City, Philippines
Completion	2011
Client	Confidential
Type of use	Living
Gross floor area	465 m²
Bamboo used	Bayog bamboo
Photos	Edward Simon

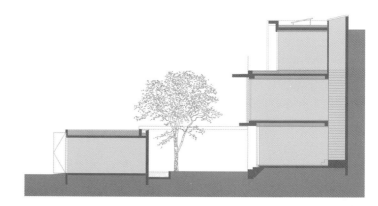

This house is located in Paranaque City, Metro Manila. The area is home to a low density neighborhood of houses and low rise buildings. The entrance foyer, garage and service area face the access road while dining, living room and kitchen overlook the private courtyard. The first floor houses a family room and a private quarter with two bedrooms, and a guest-office room with access to the roof garden. The master bedroom occupies the second floor with its own salon, changing room and bathroom. Bamboo was used for the façade, as it is a low cost material that grows locally. The bamboo poles are treated to increase their resilience and protect them from mold and pests, before being stained and varnished.

↑ Inner courtyard surrounded by water body
↓ Exterior view with rooftop terrace and canopied terrace on ground floor

↓ Entrance with bridge and view towards courtyard

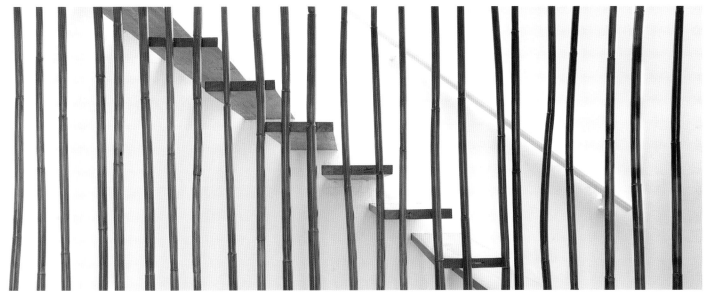

← Section
↓ Accessible rooftop behind a floating screen of bamboo poles

↑ Cantilevered wooden steps and floating bamboo poles

Bamboo Classroom Millennium School

Eleena Jamil Architect

Location	Sagnay, Philippines
Completion	2010
Client	MyShelter Foundation
Type of use	School
Gross floor area	202 m²
Bamboo used	Bambusa blumeana
Photos	Courtesy of the architects

This bamboo classroom prototype comprises two classrooms with a verandah along one side. A simple reinforced concrete frame structure defines the classroom enclosure and provides a strong anchor for the bamboo structure. The whole building is raised off the ground and topped with a large overhanging roof that ensures that teaching spaces are shaded and dry at all times. These features also help to protect the bamboo from getting wet as moisture normally renders it susceptible to rot and attack from insects. The bamboo structure is standardized and arranged repetitively along a regular system of gridlines.

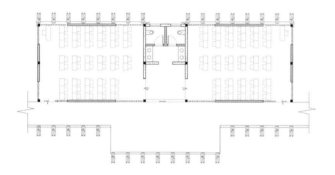

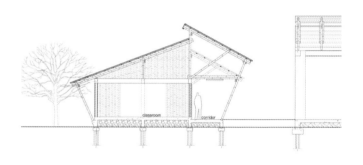

↑ Ground floor plan
↓ Front of classroom with verandah

↑ Section

↑ Bamboo connection detail
↓ Woven mat ceiling

↑ View from verandah

The Drop

Bamboo DNA

Location	Idanha a Velha, Portugal
Completion	2010
Client	Good Mood, LDA
Type of use	Art gallery
Gross floor area	2,500 m²
Bamboo used	Dendrocalamus asper, Guadua angustifolia
Photos	Gerard Minakawa

The Drop was a meandering, curvilinear art gallery created by Bamboo DNA's team and festival volunteers over the course of six weeks in Idanha a Velha, Portugal. The walls were built with wide woven bamboo panels. Each panel was woven on the ground, lifted with a reach fork, and then carefully placed into trenches. Using rope "reins", each panel was then pulled and curved inward until the right angle was achieved. Once the entire tunnel was curved and formed, bamboo roof beams were attached, locking all the curves into place. Recycled fabrics filled the spaces left in the roof canopy to protect people from the harsh summer sun.

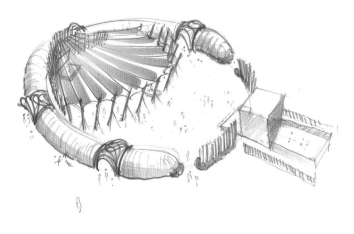

↑ Sketch
↓ Art gallery illuminated at night

↑ Public space at night

↑ Bamboo walls displaying artwork
↓ Roof canopy providing shade

↑ Bamboo support

River Safari

DP Architects

Location	Singapore, Singapore
Completion	2012
Client	Singapore Zoological Gardens
Type of use	Zoo
Gross floor area	26,936 m²
Bamboo used	Treated moso bamboo
Photos	Courtesy of the architects

Sited along the Upper Seletar Reservoir and nestled between Singapore Zoo and Night Safari, this attraction houses animals from eight freshwater habitats from around the world. A spiral staircase carved out of the structure unifies the collection of multi-functional spaces over two stories. As one traverses the veiled staircase, direct views of the surrounding nature and reservoir gradually unfold. Applying extensive treated bamboo screening underneath transforms the otherwise solid metal roofs of the huts into a lightweight canopy. The four metal roofs are supported with a cluster of twisting structural steel columns that terminates at the apex with a circular skylight.

← Spiral staircase | ↑ Sketch
↓ Site plan | → Two-story huts at entrance

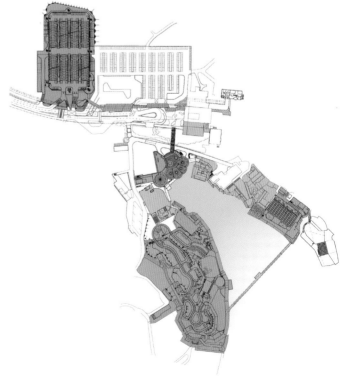

↑ Huts with natural surroundings
↓ Bamboo screening underneath the roof

↑ Walkway for visitors
↗ Open-air wash basins surrounded by bamboo and greenery

Ring of Celestial Bliss

J. J. Pan & Partners, Architects & Planners

Location	Hsinchu, Taiwan
Completion	2013
Client	Delta Electronics Foundation
Type of use	Public space
Gross floor area	3,980 m²
Bamboo used	Makino bamboo
Photos	Delta, courtesy of the architects (p. 125 a. r., 125 b.)

The choice of form and materials used for the lantern was inspired by the historical and cultural characteristics of Hsinchu, whose ancient name was the "City of Bamboo Walls." While reusable steal is the primary structural component, the outer cladding consists of bamboo trunks. The inner projection screen is made of recycled materials, and bamboo tubes are used as a permeable flooring material. The bamboo will be collected at the end of the festival and donated to the "Earth Passengers" workshop to build environmental education classrooms in Taitung. The locally sourced construction materials have the additional advantage of being environment-friendly with a reduced carbon emissions footprint.

↑ Aerial view at night
↓ Outer cladding of bamboo stems

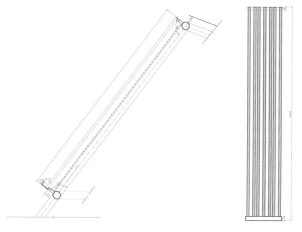

↑ Section and bamboo elevation

↑ Entire view
↓ Projection screen in use

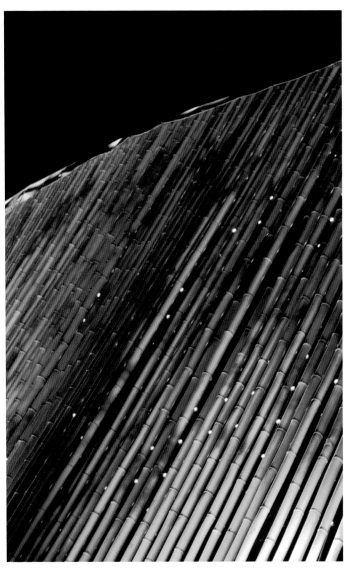

↑ Bamboo wall illuminated in various colors

Cicada

Casagrande Laboratory

Location Taipei, Taiwan
Completion 2011
Client Jut Land Development Group
Type of use Public space
Gross floor area 270 m²
Bamboo used Winter bamboo
Photos AdDa Zei

Cicada, by Finnish architect and environmental artist Marco Casagrande, is a cocoon-like spatial installation in a highly industrial region of Taipei, Taiwan. The organic bamboo structure is 34 meters in length, an inhabitable shady shelter located in the midst of bus roads and traffic infrastructure. Woven into a simple crisscross structure, the bamboo forms a permeable shell, sunlight filters through creating a gentle play of light and shadow. Cicada is a public space for visitors, encompassing a central fireplace underneath an aperture in the roof. Small benches provide flexible seating along the length of the installation.

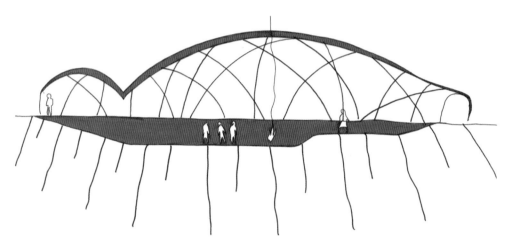

↑ Sketch
↓ Central fire place

↑ General view
↓ Entrance area

↑ Interior path accompanied by bamboo walls
↓ Interior view

↑ Cicada creates a shady shelter
↗ Wall in detail

Chalachol Terminal 21

NKDW

Location	Bangkok, Thailand
Completion	2012
Client	Chalachol
Type of use	Hair salon
Gross floor area	107 m²
Bamboo used	Rough giant bamboo
Photos	Nattapon Klinsuwan

This project investigates the question of what a city needs to enable it to survive in the future. Nattapon Klinsuwan of NKDW has come up with a design that promotes the idea of a 'green' city and economic growth. This salon appears to be wrapped by numerous bamboo sticks hanging from the ceiling at different levels throughout the space. Klinsuwan designed the space as a sculpture that people can walk through and look around, making them question what they are seeing. Instead of creating walls or partitions to separate working areas, the designer divides them by using different lengths of bamboo sticks hanging down from the ceiling. Some poles are long enough to touch the floor, which helps to blur the line between wall and ceiling.

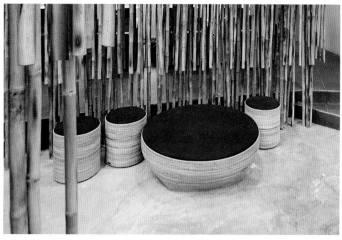

↑ Seating in front of bamboo wall
↓ Ceiling detail

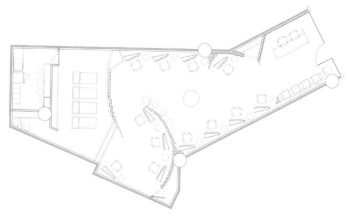

↑ Furniture layout plan

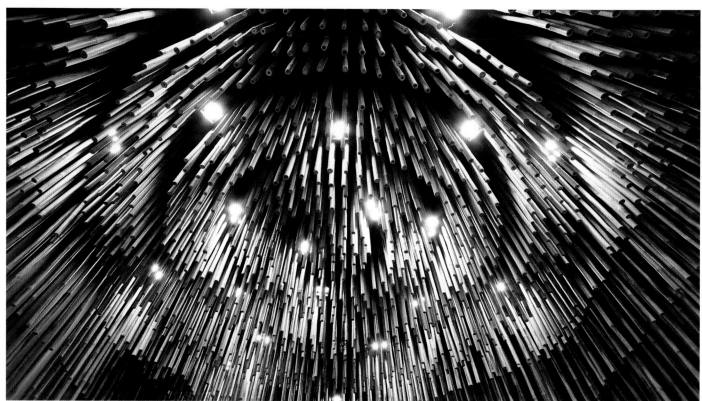

↑ Main entrance area
↓ Bamboo poles in various lengths

↑ Styling area
↓ Seating and mirrors

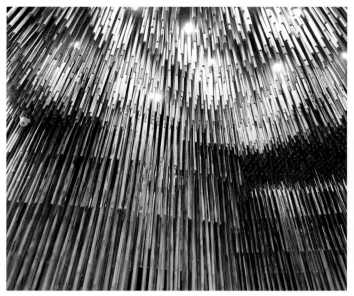

↑ Bamboo sticks hanging on different levels
→ Bamboo walls create partitions

Library in Thailand

Rintala Eggertsson Architects, TYIN tegnestue Architects

Location	Ban Tha Song Yang, Thailand
Completion	2009
Client	Safe Haven Orphanage
Type of use	Library
Gross floor area	28 m²
Photos	Pasi Aalto

This project is the result of a workshop held at the Safe Haven Orphanage in Ban Tha Song Yang, Thailand in January 2009. TYIN tegnestue Architects invited Sami Rintala and 15 Norwegian architecture students from the Norwegian University of Technology and Science (NTNU) to participate in the completion of a new library for the orphanage. The concrete base of the library is cast on a bed of large rocks gathered on-site. Walls made of plastered concrete blocks cool the building during the day, while the open bamboo façade provides good ventilation. The new building offers the Safe Haven Orphanage a library and study area and is also a gathering space, frequently used for play, games and crafts.

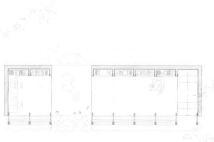

↑ Ground floor plan
↓ Playground and seating behind library

↑ Front elevation

↑ Bookshelves
↓ Computer area for studying

↑ Entrance to library

Panyaden School

24H > architecture

Location	Chiang Mai, Thailand
Completion	2011
Client	Yodphet Sudsawad
Type of use	School
Gross floor area	5,000 m²
Bamboo used	Various
Photos	Ally Taylor

In lush green surroundings, where Thailand's highest mountains meet the flat rice fields, Panyaden School contracted 24H>architecture to design its environmentally friendly school buildings. This primary school consists of an informal arrangement of pavilions (salas), organized along pathways inspired by the shape of the tropical antler horn fern. The classroom pavilions have load-bearing walls of rammed earth, dividing the buildings into three classrooms. Columns consist of bamboo bundles reaching up to the bamboo canopy from their stone foundations. The school has been built from local earth and local bamboo that has been naturally treated to withstand the elements. Wastewater treatment and food waste recycling round up the picture of an environmentally friendly school with a negligible carbon footprint.

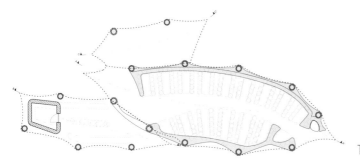

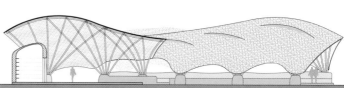

↑ Plan
↓ Roof supported by bamboo

↑ Section

↑ Pathways connect the buildings
↓ Large pavilion

↑ Pavilions protect from sun and rain
↓ Children's playground

↑ School surrounded by rice fields and mountains
→ Bird's-eye view of pavilions

The Hut

Bambooroo

Location	Chiang Mai, Thailand
Completion	2013
Client	Sabu Sabu
Type of use	Guesthouse
Gross floor area	36 m²
Bamboo used	Dendrocalamus
Photos	Marisa Marchitelli

Sabu Sabu, an organic handmade soap company, requested a private accommodation unit where clients from out of town could stay overnight. Bamboo architects from Bambooroo were engaged to design and construct The Hut, a boutique bamboo bungalow guesthouse in Chiang Mai, Northern Thailand. Unique and comfortable in its design, this structure is located alongside the rice paddy fields, with views across the agricultural land-scape and of a distant mountain range. A long bench wraps around the perimeter of the deck arranged in the traditional Thai sala configuration. The Hut is the perfect hide-away for writers, artists, meditators and nature lovers, as well as those who seek a quiet and exclusive place to get away from it all.

↑ Hut surrounded by greenery
↓ Rear side terrace with seating

↑ Elevation

↑ Bamboo furniture
↓ Guesthouse entrance

↑ View from bedroom to terrace

Ecological Children Activity and Education Center

24H > architecture

Location	Koh Kood, Thailand
Completion	2009
Client	Six Senses Resorts and Spas
Type of use	Leisure, education
Gross floor area	165 m^2
Bamboo used	Dendracolamus asper, Bambusa multiplex
Photos	Boris Zeisser, Kiattipong Panchee (p. 145)

The six-star Soneva Kiri resort is located on an island in the Gulf of Thailand. 24H > architecture have designed a series of ecological icons to contribute to Six Senses' high ambitions in design and ecology. Most prominent is The Children Activity and Education Center, which will provide visiting children a wide range of entertaining activities. "The Den" provides an auditorium or cinema for films, lectures and plays, a library with books on permaculture and local traditions, an art room, a music room and fashion room. The structure and roof of "The Den" are made from local Thai bamboo, thus contributing to the ecological approach of the resort. The interior is made from local plantation River Red Gum wood and rattan structural elements. The roof provides shade and offers protection from the heavy rains.

↑ Roof protects children from sunlight
↓ Lighting at night

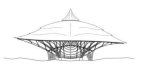

↑ Elevations and sections
→ Building located on slope

↑ Reading corner
↓ Colorful play spaces

↑ Interior
→ Bamboo support

MOVINGschool 001

Building Trust International

Location   Mae Sot, Thailand
Completion   2012
Client   Migrant Education
Design team   Amadeo Bennetta, Dan LaRossa
Type of use   School
Gross floor area 215 m²
Bamboo used   Dendrocalamus giganteus
Photos   Louise Cole

In 2011, Building Trust International launched an International design competition asking architects, designers and engineers to come up with an innovative design solution for a mobile, modular school for a displaced community of migrants and refugees on the border between Thailand and Myanmar. Building Trust International constructed the winning design in collaboration with Ironwood Studio, a social enterprise in Mae Sot that provided local apprentices to carry out the metal work for the steel frame construction and carpentry skills needed to create the bamboo wall panels. The design maximizes the use of traditional bamboo building techniques for the walls and solar blinds.

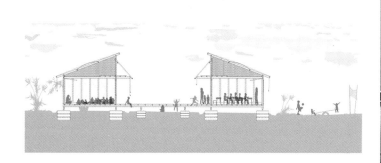

↑ Section
↓ Construction diagram

↑ Open plan classroom

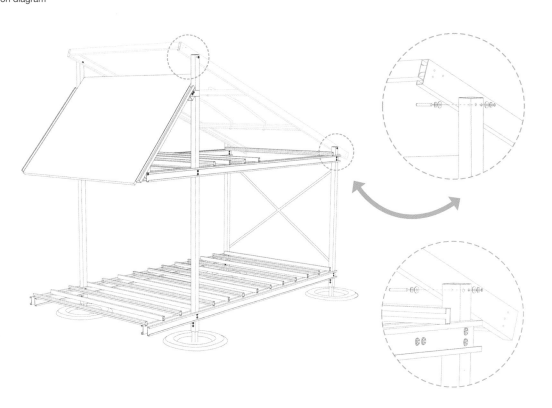

↑ Pupils in front of school buildings
↓ Corridor between walls and bamboo blinds

↑ Exterior view of school buildings

Temporary Dormitories of CDC School

a.gor.a architects

Location   Mae Sot, Thailand
Completion   2012
Client   Mae Tao Clinic
Type of use   Dormitories
Gross floor area   72 m²
Bamboo used   Dendrocalamus asper
Photos   Allyse Pulliam, Franc-Pallarès López
               (pp. 149, 150 a., 151 b.)

These temporary dormitories are located in Mae Sot, Thailand and are the result of a collaboration between Albert Company Olmo, Jan Glasmeier and the construction company Gyaw Gyaw. The armed conflict in Myanmar has resulted in a large number of refugees crossing the border into neighboring Thailand. Numerous schools and orphanages have sprung up along the border and one of these, the Child Development Center under the tutelage of Mae Tao Clinic, accommodates more than 500 students. These dormitories are a low-cost and easy to assemble solution that provides the center with more space to house the ever-increasing number of children. The first four dormitories were built within a time frame of just four weeks and are open, light and airy, offering semi-private living space for up to three students.

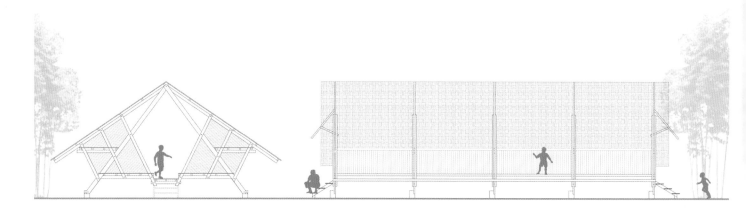

↑ Elevation and section
↓ Entrance to one of the dormitories

↑ Dormitory at dawn with illuminated internal corridor
↓ Ensemble of buildings

↑ Roof decking made from eucalyptus leaves
↓ Entrance situation from inside

↑ Dormitory occupied by migrant children
↓ Entrance area and central corridor

Soe Ker Tie House

TYIN tegnestue Architects

Location	Noh Bo, Thailand
Completion	2009
Client	Ole Jorgen Edna
Type of use	Living
Gross floor area	12.8 m²
Photos	Pasi Aalto

In the fall of 2008 TYIN travelled to Noh Bo, a small village on the Thai-Burmese border to design and build houses for Karen refugee children. The 60 year long conflict in Burma has left many children orphaned. The main driving force behind the Soe Ker Tie House was to provide the children with their own space, a place that they could call home. The most prominent feature is the bamboo weaving technique, which was used on the sides and at the rear of the houses. All of the bamboo was harvested within a few kilometers of the site. The specially shaped roofs promote natural ventilation within the sleeping units. To prevent problems with moisture and rot, the sleeping units are raised off the ground on four concrete foundations, cast in old tires.

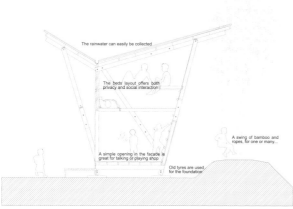

The rainwater can easily be collected

The beds layout offers both privacy and social interaction

A simple opening in the facade is great for talking or playing shop

A swing of bamboo and ropes, for one or many...

Old tyres are used for the foundation

↑ Section
↓ Three different window solutions

↑ Site plan

↑ Overlapping levels encourage play and communication
↓ Space with barbeque and seating

↑ Colorful window
↓ Drained pathway in front of the houses

↑ Interior space with transparency to the outside
→ Space for play on ground floor

Botanica Condominium Sales Gallery

Vin Varavarn Architects

Location	Pak Chong, Thailand
Completion	2012
Client	Scenical Developments Co., Ltd.
Interior design	Define Studio
Type of use	Condominium sales gallery
Gross floor area	358 m²
Bamboo used	Gramineae bamboo
Photos	Spaceshift Studio

The Botanica Condominium Sales Gallery is located close to the famous Khao Yai National Park Thailand. The design reflects a desire to harmonize architecture with the beautiful natural environment. The architecture is simple, a solution that helps to enhance rather than overpower the natural beauty of the landscape. This group of buildings comprises a sales office, two showroom buildings and toilet facilities, all connected by an outdoor elevated walkway through open natural landscape. The two showrooms are finished with bamboo paneling sprayed with glossy black paint. A second steel roof structure with bamboo slats has been installed to screen off the intense light from the skylight.

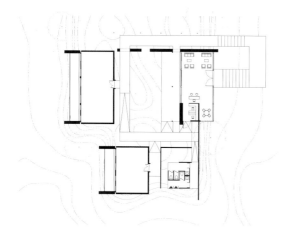

↑ Site plan
↓ Entrance to sales office

↑ Conceptual sketch of inner court
→ Straight structural lines contrast natural surroundings

↑ Solid boxes covered with black bamboo
↓ Bamboo roof

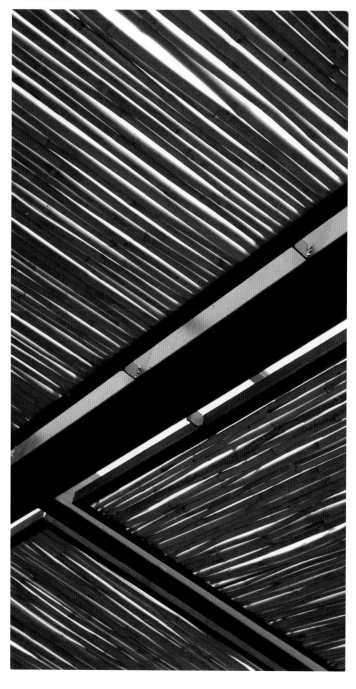

↑ Pattern of sunlight through bamboo roof
↓ Black bamboo wall contrasts natural surroundings

Bamboo Starscraper

Bamboo DNA

Location	Indio, CA, USA
Completion	2009
Client	Goldenvoice
Type of use	Festival landmark
Gross floor area	870 m²
Bamboo used	Dendrocalamus asper, Guadua angustifolia
Photos	Jeff Clark, Nils Hammerbeck (p. 160 r.)

The Bamboo Starscraper gets its name from the six-sided star-shape upon which the entire structural plan was based. Six bamboo poles were lashed together to create a simple but elegant cross bracing system. Seen from below, any viewer can recognize the six-pointed star at the tower's heart. A concentric series of bamboo columns are held in tension by synthetic aramid fiber rope, which is stronger than steel. A gas-fueled flaming spire tops off the entire piece, suspended only by aramid fiber rope. The Bamboo Starscraper was structurally engineered to withstand 145-kilometer per hour wind gusts, the strictest requirements in the country.

↑ Illumination at night
↓ Diagram

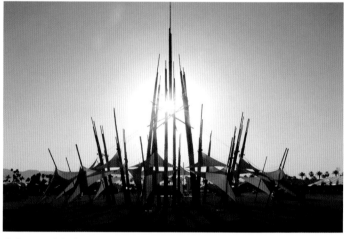

↑ Pattern of shadow created by sunlight
↓ Perspective

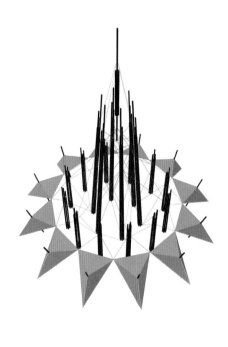

↑ Top of tower seen from below
↓ Construction of bamboo poles, ropes and fabric

↑ Flaming spire

Mason Lane Farm Operations Facility

De Leon & Primmer Architecture Workshop

Location	Louisville, KY, USA
Completion	2009
Client	Eleanor Bingham Miller
Type of use	Agriculture
Gross floor area	1,550 m²
Bamboo used	Yellow groove bamboo
Photos	Courtesy of the architects

The Mason Lane Farm Operations Facility is a new complex for farm equipment servicing, re-fueling and storage, as well as providing seasonal storage for grain and hay. The facility supports a 8.1-square-kilometer property utilized for agriculture, recreation, wildlife habitat and conservation purposes. The facility's barn buildings explore the potential of conventional construction systems, utilizing prefabricated framing elements and locally sourced materials. A 'reductive' design approach is implemented in the deliberate expression of material and constructional layering. The LEED-certified project focuses on 'low-tech' passive sustainable strategies that are based on a nuanced understanding of site and local climate.

↑ Interior view of barn B
↓ Bamboo façade seen from north

↑ Site plan

↑ Bamboo lattice detail
↓ Arrangement of buildings

↑ Equipment storage area in barn A

Da Nang Bamboo Gridshell

David Rockwood, Architect

Location	Da Nang City, Vietnam
Completion	2012
Type of use	Education
Gross floor area	230 m²
Bamboo used	Bambusa blumeana
Photos	Phuong Ngo

This structure is the last in a series of experimental structures produced to test the viability of bamboo for gridshell structures. The objective was to produce an 'hourglass' form at least 12 meters in width and 20 meters in length that could accommodate a variety of different functions. The Da Nang Bamboo Gridshell was assembled on the ground, starting with arranging a first layer of built-up split bamboo members, laying down a second layer directly on top of the first, and lashing these together at nodal points. The structure was then lifted at the center, and pushed inward from the edges to spring it into position. A tensed fabric membrane covers the structure, protecting it from the weather and increasing lateral load resistance.

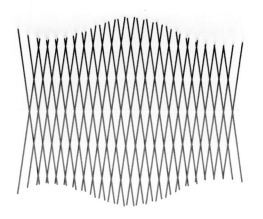

↑ Diagram of gridshell laid-out flat
↓ Forming of 'hourglass' double curvature

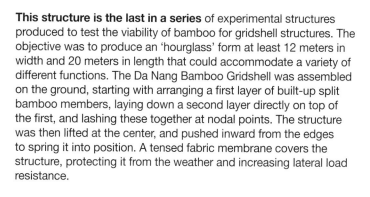

↑ Sketch

↑ Testing lateral load resistance
↓ Assembly

↑ Splitting bamboo
↓ Base connection detail

↑ Springing gridshell into final position
→ Gridshell base

Blooming Bamboo Home

H&P Architects

Location	Hanoi, Vietnam
Completion	2013
Client	Hoang Van Duy
Type of use	Various
Gross floor area	44 m²
Photos	Doan Thanh Ha

The climate in Vietnam can be tough and a range of natural phenomena regularly cause catastrophes. The damage caused by drought, floods, landslides and storms can have a significant impact on communities and the need to find a quick and affordable housing solution is of paramount importance. The Blooming Bamboo Home seeks to provide easy to assemble homes strong enough to withstand certain weather conditions, such as a one-and-a-half meter flood. The space is multi-functional and can be used as a home, classroom, medical center, or community center. The house can be built by the users, without any need for expert assistance and can be constructed within a time frame of just 25 days.

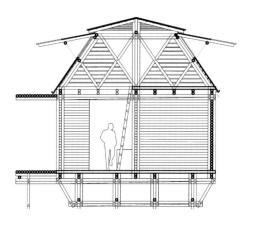

↑ Section
↓ Bamboo roof

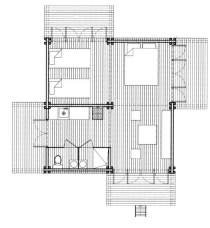

↑ Ground floor plan

↑ Façade with greenery
↓ Interior with bamboo seating

↑ View at night

BES Pavilion

H&P Architects

Location   Ha Tinh City, Vietnam
Completion   2013
Client   Nguyen Van Quang
Type of use   Community space
Gross floor area   123 m²
Photos   Tran Tuan Trung

The Bamboo Earth and Stone (BES) pavilion is a community space that focuses on promoting art and culture. Located in the center of Ha Tinh City, BES is built from local materials, constructed using traditional building methods. The cluster comprises various separated areas, which are arranged freely around a central courtyard; here, the use of bamboo creates an interesting play of light and shadow. The building functions as a communal, cultural space, bringing people together and promoting dialogue.

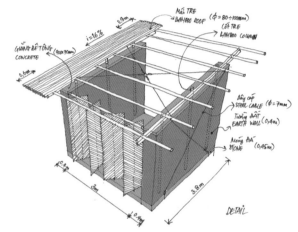

↑ Bamboo interior and seating
↓ Open central courtyard

↑ Diagram

↑ Pavilions provide sheltered space
↓ View from street

↑ Courtyard with greenery

Kontum Indochine Café

Vo Trong Nghia Architects

Location	Kontum, Vietnam
Completion	2013
Client	Truong Long JSC
Type of use	Café
Gross floor area	551 m²
Bamboo used	Iron bamboo
Photos	Hiroyuki Oki

Kontum Indochine Café is designed as a part of a hotel complex along Dakbla River in Kontum City, Central Vietnam. Located on a corner plot, the café is composed of two major elements: a main building with a big horizontal roof made of bamboo structure and an annex kitchen made of concrete frames and stones. The bamboo roof provides ample shade and maximizes the flow of cool air coming from surface of the nearby lake. This eliminates the need for air conditioning inside, even in a tropical climate. The roof is covered by fiber-reinforced plastic panels and thatch. The translucent synthetic panels are partly exposed in the ceiling to provide natural light in the deep center of the space under the roof.

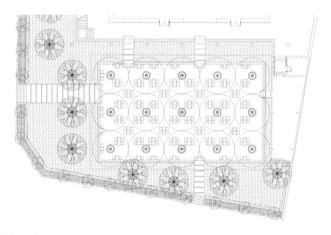

↑ Floor plan
↓ Seating area shaded by bamboo roof

↑ Building surrounded by artificial pond and trees
→ Reflections in water

↑ Cafeteria with V-shaped roof
↓ Path leading to entrance

↑ Natural lighting through translucent roof
↗ Lighting and reflections at night

Bamboo Wing

Vo Trong Nghia Architects

Location	Vinhphuc, Vietnam
Completion	2009
Client	Hong Hac Dai Lai JSC
Type of use	Café, restaurant
Gross floor area	1,430 m²
Bamboo used	Iron bamboo
Photos	Hiroyuki Oki

In an idyllic natural setting near Hanoi, Bamboo Wing is a pure bamboo cantilevered structure that hangs in the air like outstretched wings. The aim of the project was to study bamboo, not only as a finishing material but as a structural one. The 12-meter-wide structure is balanced on one rear leg, this creates an extensive space beneath that can be used to host local events such as fashion shows, live music and conferences. The only structural materials used were bamboo and stainless steel wire, which helps to protect the roof from storms. Bamboo Wing was not only a structural adventure, it also promotes the use of ecological materials, which are readily available in Vietnam.

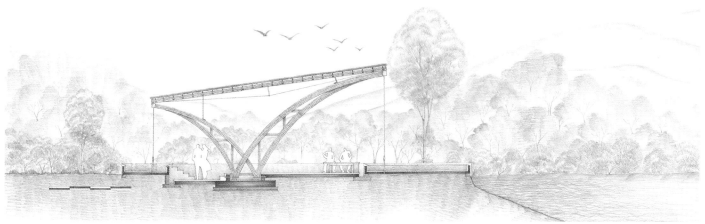

↑ Section
↓ Seating area with view of trees and pond

→ Cantilevered bamboo structure

↑ 12-meter-wide bamboo structure
↓ Lighting and reflections at night

↑ Building as part of the surrounding nature
↓ Restaurant with seating at night

Architects' Index

24H > architecture
Hoflaan 132
3062 JM Rotterdam
The Netherlands
www.24h.eu
→ 136, 142

a.gor.a architects
798/2, Intarakiri Road, Soi 40
Mae Sot 63110, Thailand
www.agora-architects.com
→ 148

Advanced Architecture Lab [AaL]
No. 1 Floor 12, Guanggu Financial
Harbour B5 building
Wuhan Donghu New Technology
Development Zone, China
www.aa-lab.org
→ 052

Arcgency
Gasværksvej 8d, 1
1656 Copenhagen V, Denmark
www.arcgency.com
→ 054

ARCò - architettura e cooperazione
Via Friuli 26/A
20135 Milan, Italy
www.ar-co.org
→ 112

Ryuichi Ashizawa Architects & associates
Floor 3 Nakajima-Building
1-1-4 Nakazaki-nishi, Kita-ku
Osaka 530-0015, Japan
www.r-a-architects.com
→ 094

AST 77 architects and engineering bvba.
Goossensvest 45
3300 Tienen, Belgium
www.ast77.be
→ 008

Atelier Bow-Wow
8-79, Suga-cho, Shinjuku-ku
Tokyo 160-0018, Japan
www.bow-wow.jp
→ 076

AZPML Ltd.
55 Curtain Road
London EC2A 3PT
United Kingdom
www.azpml.com
→ 038

Bamboo DNA
2105 Refugio Road
Goleta, CA 93117, USA
www.bamboodna.com
→ 084, 118, 160

Bambooroo
7 Shiprock Road
Port Hacking
2229 Sydney, Australia
www.bambooroo.net
→ 140

Building Trust International
1 The Street
Westmeston, Hassocks, Sussex
BN6 8RJ, United Kingdom
www.buildingtrustinternational.org
→ 146

Studio Cardenas Conscious Design
Corso di Porta Nuova 11
20121 Milan, Italy
www.studiocardenas.it
→ 086, 088

Casagrande Laboratory
Puolukkakatu 4
10300 Karjaa, Finland
www.clab.fi
→ 048, 126

Conbam
An der Vogelstange 40
52511 Geilenkirchen, Germany
www.bambus-conbam.de
→ 106

Atelier Sacha Cotture
Floor 8 Chemphil Building, 851 A
Arnaiz Avenue
Legaspi Village, Makati City
1227 Philippines
www.ateliersachacotture.com
→ 114

De Leon & Primmer
Architecture Workshop
117 South Shelby Street
Louisville, KY 40202, USA
www.deleon-primmer.com
→ 162

Define Studio
235/24 Sukhumvit 31
Klongtannuea Wattana
Bangkok 10110, Thailand
www.definestudio.com
→ 156

Design C
Enkay Center, Block A
Udyog Vihar Phase V
Gurgaon 122016, Haryana, India
→ 042

Ifigeneia Dilaveraki
Argolidos 26
11523 Athens, Greece
www.ifidil.com
→ 106

DP Architects
6 Raffles Boulevard
#04-100 Marina Square
039594, Singapore
www.dpa.com.sg
→ 120

DSA+s
Surya Permata 2 blok 3G/9
Sunrise Garden, Jakarta Barat
11520, Indonesia
www.dspacearchitect.com
→ 080

Galeazzo Design
Rua Antonio Bicudo 83 Pinheiros
05418-010 São Paulo, Brazil
www.fabiogaleazzo.com.br
→ 012. 020, 024

Elena Goray
Plantage Doklaan 42/3
1018 CN Amsterdam
The Netherlands
www.elenagoray.com
→ 106

H&P Architects
Floor 2, Building B8-TT18
Bach Thai Buoi Street
Van Quan Urban Zone,
Ha Dong District, Vietnam
www.hpa.vn
→ 168, 170

Helen&Hard
Vindmøllebakken 2
4014 Stavanger, Norway
www.helenhard.no
→ 044

HPP Architekten
Kaistraße 5
40221 Düsseldorf, Germany
www.hpp.com
→ 064

HWCD
Room 704-705, L'Avenue
99 Xianxia Road
Shanghai, China
www.h-w-c-d.com
→ 056

Integer Ltd
14F Malaysia Buidling
50 Gloucester Road
Hong Kong, China
www.integerasia.org
→ 028, 034

Eleena Jamil Architect
Unit 07-02, Jalan Su 1E
Persiaran Sering Ukay
68000 Ampang, Selangor, Malaysia
www.ej-architect.com
→ 116

Architects' Index

Komitu Architects
Kalevankatu 31 A 9
00100 Helsinki, Finland
www.komituarchitects.org
→ 026

Kengo Kuma & Associates
2-24-8 BY-CUBE 2F
Minamiaoyama, Minato-ku
Tokyo 107-0062, Japan
www.kkaa.co.jp
→ 090, 096

MA (Manasaram Architects)
7 Aditi Greenscapes
20, Venkateshpura
Bangalore 560077, India
www.manasaramarchitects.com
→ 068, 070

NKDW
40/2 Suksawat 2
Suksawat Road Chom-Thon
Bangkok 10150, Thailand
www.nkdw-studio.com
→ 130

Ojtat Creatividad Regenerativa
6 Poniente 103
72810 San Andrés Cholula
Puebla, Mexico
www.ojtat.org
→ 100

**J. J. Pan & Partners,
Architects & Planners**
21, Alley 12, Lane 118
Ren Ai Road
Section 3, Taipei 10657, Taiwan
www.jjpan.com
→ 124

Sanjay Prakash & Associates
Room 1/301 Hauz Khaz Enclave
New Delhi 110016, India
www.sanjayprakash.co.in
→ 042

Sanjay Puri Architects
20 Famous Studio Lane
Off Dr. E. Moses Road
Mahalaxmi Mumbai 400011, India
www.sanjaypuriarchitects.com
→ 078

Rintala Eggertsson Architects
Hyttebakken 33 B
8011 Bodø, Norway
www.ri-eg.com
→ 134

David Rockwood, Architect
Room 1904, Kapiolani Boulevard
2439 Honolulu, HI 96826, USA
www.arch.hawaii.edu
→ 164

**Pradeep Sachdeva Design
Associates**
4 Windmill Place
Aya Nagar Village
New Delhi 110047, India
www.psda.in
→ 042, 072

Benjamin Garcia Saxe
Office 9910, PO Box 6945
London W1A 6US, United Kingdom
www.benjamingarciasaxe.com
→ 060

Studio MK27
Alameda Tietê, 505
Cerqueira César
01417-020 São Paulo, Brazil
www.studiomk27.com.br
→ 016

The Oval Partnership Ltd
Floor 14, Malaysia Buidling
50 Gloucester Road
Hong Kong, China
www.ovalpartnership.com
→ 028, 034

TYIN tegnestue Architects
Alfred Getz' vei 3
7034 Trondheim, Norway
www.tyinarchitects.com
→ 134, 152

Vector Architects
Room 1903, South Tower, SOHO
Shangdu, 8 Dongdaqiao Road
Chaoyang District
100020 Beijing, China
www.vectorarchitects.com
→ 030

Simón Vélez
→ 042, 072

Vin Varavarn Architects
89/15 Wireless Road
Lumpini, Patumwan
Bangkok 10330, Thailand
www.vva.co.th
→ 156

Vo Trong Nghia Architects
Floor 8, 70 Pham Ngoc Thach
street, Ward 6, District 3
Ho Chi Minh City, Vietnam
www.votrongnghia.com
→ 036, 172, 176

Ziegert | Roswag | Seiler
Architekten Ingenieure
Aufgang A, Schlesische Straße 26
10997 Berlin, Germany
www.zrs-berlin.de
→ 104, 108

Imprint

The Deutsche Nationalbibliothek lists this publication in the Deutsche Nationalbibliografie; detailed bibliographic data are available in the Internet at http://dnb.dnb.de

ISBN 978-3-03768-182-4

© 2015 by Braun Publishing AG
www.braun-publishing.ch

1st edition 2015

Selection of projects: Editorial office van Uffelen
Editorial staff and layout: Christina Mihajlovski, Johanna Schröder, Lisa Rogers
Translation: Lisa Rogers
Graphic concept: Manuela Roth